ideals® OLD-FASHIONED

My arms reach out through time and space
And hold each memory in place:

A creaking swing, a whispered word,
A promise only night winds heard . . .

A little footstep on the stair,
A small fragmented baby prayer.

My arms reach out through time and space
And do not find an empty place.

June Masters Bacher

Publisher, Patricia A. Pingry
Editor, Peggy Schaefer
Art Director, Patrick McRae
Production Manager, Jan Johnson
Editorial Assistant, Kathleen Gilbert
Copy Editor, Joan Anderson

Front and back covers by Gene Ahrens

Inside front cover by George Hinke
Inside back cover by Bill Hebden

ISBN 0-8249-1063-X

IDEALS—Vol. 45, No. 5 August MCMLXXXVIII IDEALS (ISSN 0019-137X) is published eight times a year,
February, March, May, June, August, September, November, December
by IDEALS PUBLISHING CORPORATION, Nelson Place at Elm Hill Pike, Nashville, Tenn. 37214
Second class postage paid at Nashville, Tennessee, and additional mailing offices.
Copyright © MCMLXXXVIII by IDEALS PUBLISHING CORPORATION.
POSTMASTER: Send address changes to Ideals, Post Office Box 148000, Nashville, Tenn. 37214-8000
All rights reserved. Title IDEALS registered U.S. Patent Office.

SINGLE ISSUE—$3.95
ONE-YEAR SUBSCRIPTION—eight consecutive issues as published—$17.95
TWO-YEAR SUBSCRIPTION—sixteen consecutive issues as published—$31.95
Outside U.S.A., add $6.00 per subscription year for postage and handling.

The cover and entire contents of IDEALS are fully protected by copyright and must
not be reproduced in any manner whatsoever. Printed and bound in U.S.A.

A Song

Ella Wheeler

Is anyone sad in the world, I wonder?
    Does anyone weep on a day like this?
With the sun above, and the green earth under,
    Why, what is life but a dream of bliss?

With sun, and the skies, and the birds above me,
    Birds that sing as they wheel and fly—
With the winds to follow and say they love me—
    Who could be lonely? Oh no, not I!

One who claims that he knows about it
    Tells me the earth is a vale of sin;
But I, and the bees, and the birds—we doubt it,
    And think it a world worth living in.

I told the thrush, and we laughed together,
    Laughed till the woods were all a-ring;
And he said to me, as he plumed each feather,
    "Well, people must croak, if they cannot sing."

Up he flew, but his song remaining
    Rang like a bell in my heart all day,
And silenced the voices of weak complaining
    That pipe like insects along the way.

Photo Opposite
FLOWERS OF SUMMER
Comstock, Inc.

Photo Overleaf
GRAND TETON NATIONAL PARK
Larry Burton

Built to Endure

Gladys Taber

This was a house of homespun living, but one has the feeling it was happy living. It is strange how houses affect one. Some houses, old or new, seem to breathe a serene air. Some, for no good reason at all, seem depressing. Now and then I go into a house that suddenly makes me feel chilled, and I know several houses which give me a sense of brightness even if I am melancholy when I enter.

There is no reason to think houses cannot have their own personality, and they do. In an old house, the living that has gone on within the walls adds character; in a modern ranch house, it might be the reflection of the architect's mood, I suppose.

Old houses were built soundly, built to endure. But now and then things happen to them. Our friends Lois and Burt Klakring were about to buy an old house not long ago. They were just ready to close the deal when the real estate agent took them down to the cellar to see the furnace.

"And one thing you can be sure of," he said proudly, "these old beams are as sound as ever." He took a penknife from his pocket and stuck it in one of the great foundation beams.

Whereupon the knife sank to the hilt, soft powder began to drift out, and the beam ominously cracked open. They all ran for their lives, Lois said. They made it, but it was a near thing.

So they got a modern house in the end.

With a modern house you begin the traditions, I feel, but with an old house, you inherit them.

Photo Opposite
VICTORIAN HOUSE
HERMANN, MISSOURI
Robert Lee II

Daisies of the Field

Joy Belle Burgess

Coy little daisies, you honor the hill
With your beauty which kindles the joy you impart;
And where the vast field knows the wide open sky,
You grow in profusion and capture my heart.

On tall, leafy stems you quiver and sway,
Bent by a zephyr, soft whisper of breeze,
And cast a bright glow with your snow-white rays,
While so shyly you seem to smile and tease.

You captivate me with your pungent smell
That permeates the field and the cloudless sky,
That tingles my nose as I breathe in deep,
And leaves spellbound and weak a passing butterfly.

How free of all care, how peaceful your mood.
If only I could share you with troubled humankind;
For with just one glimpse of this snow-white field,
Anxieties would flee and there'd be peace of mind.

I'll drink in this beauty, then tell all I meet
How inspiring these flowers that beautify the sod,
That wait to uplift all who walk by the way.
How dear are the daisies that glorify God.

General Store

Rosaline Guingrich

Gone with the years is the general store
With its bell that rang when you opened the door.
The store was a clutter of everything
From hardware to groceries, cloth, and string;

Shelved were the calicos, ginghams, and lace,
Shoes, pants, and flannels all crowded in space.
The counters were made substantial and wide
With bins for spilly-like things inside;

On one stood the scales, the coffee, the tea,
Another held pots, pans, and crockery.
A barrel of crackers sat close to the cheese
Tempting the public to munch at their ease;

Baskets of sundries arrested the eye
While rubber boots, brooms, and lanterns hung high.
Though stock was as varied as it could be,
The showcase with candy inveigled me.

Lucky the child with a penny or two
For peppermint sticks and licorice, too.
The potbellied stove was a favorite lair
With its spittoon, checkerboard, bench, and chair

Way back where the loaders sat and sat
To spin their yarns while they spat and spat.
What fanciful tales the menfolk could tell
Who traded at stores with the ringing bell.

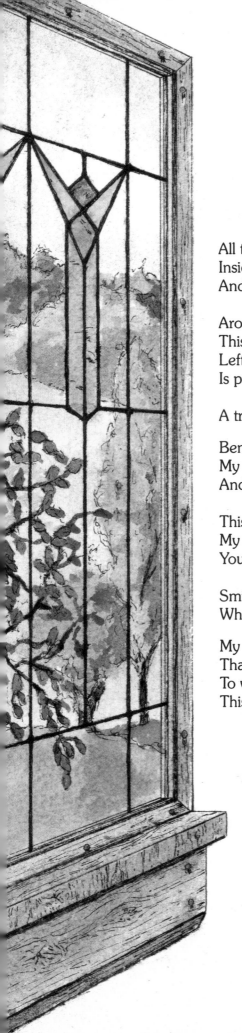

Readers'

Gran's Legacy

Judy Robertson Ellis

All tucked away in Gran's old chest,
Inside a velvet box at rest
And wrapped in lace with tissue
     spread
Around it gently like a web,
This sentimental legacy
Left years ago by Gran for me
Is priceless, yes, worth more than
     gold,
A treasure that I dare to hold.

Beneath the lace and tissue fine,
My fingers trace familiar lines
And peeking out, one clear blue
     eye—
This china doll brings me delight.
My Gran's own dollie, worn and old,
You're cheeks shine bright from
     kisses stole,
Smiling still like yesterday
When Gran would let us sit and play.

My Gran, she knew I loved you best.
That's why she put you here to rest,
To wait until I came to find
This secret place—
     Just Gran's and mine.

A Patchwork of Memories

Hildagarde Smith Madahgian

Memories of my childhood
Are like a patchwork quilt;
Jumbled scenes shuffle around
Till one design is built.

The big log house forms the
     background
For sketches from the past;
The fireplace and the warm lamplight
Are pictures that will last.

The stove 'round which we gathered
On dark, cold winter morns,
The organ and the phonograph
With records old and worn;

The orchard on the hillside,
White blossoms in the spring,
Hollyhocks for summer days,
Tall pines where robins sing;

The big red barn and barnyard,
The cows brought home each night,
Lush green pastures down the lane,
The clear creek sparkling bright;

This beautiful patchwork of memories
Is a lovely design, you see.
I may have left the country life,
But the memories will never leave me

Editor's Note: Readers are invited to submit unpublished, original poetry, short anecdotes, and humorous reflections on life for possible publication in future *Ideals* issues. Please send copies only; manuscripts will not be returned. Writers will receive $10 for each published submission. Send materials to "Readers' Reflections," Ideals Publishing Corporation, Nelson Place at Elm Hill Pike, Nashville, Tennessee 37214.

Reflections

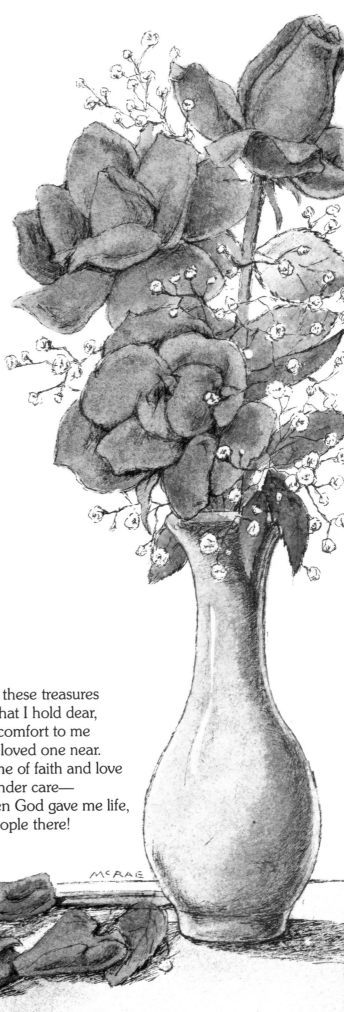

Life Is Too Short

Shirley Pope Waite

The older I get, the more I realize that life is too short to fret about
    frayed washcloths
    burned cookies
    cat hair on the couch
    the ring in the bathtub
    the woman who barged ahead in the grocery line
    the car repair bills
    the cutting remark by my relative.
The older I get, the more I realize that life is too short to postpone
    telling my friend how much I appreciate her
    writing that overdue letter
    finishing the children's scrapbooks
    doing those stomach-firming exercises
    reading the entire Bible in that new version
    writing the poem that's been on my mind
    volunteering to babysit for my young neighbor.
The older I get, the more I realize that life is too short.

Treasures

Carol E. Nieves

Grandma's crystal candy jar
With sun rays sparkling through,
A quaint handpainted pitcher,
A slender vase of blue—
All bring thoughts of people gone
And the childhood I once knew.
These old things give more joy to me
Than new ones ever do.

As I muse upon these treasures
From the folks that I hold dear,
They give such comfort to me
That I feel each loved one near.
They speak to me of faith and love
And of much tender care—
I'm grateful when God gave me life,
He put good people there!

Flat Land

Edna Jaques

I love flat land, flat as a table top,
    Holding upon its breast a growing crop
Of oats or barley, wheat in serried rows,
    A trailing buckwheat vine that often grows
Amid the wheat as if to give it grace,
    Like a print apron with a frill of lace.

Deep bottomland they call it, fields that hold
    The heavy strength of loam and peaty mold,
Rich earth to feed the roots of growing stuff,
    Stout trunks with branches sinewy and tough,
And tender leaves veined like a baby's hand
    Drawing their strength and beauty from the land.

I love flat land where quiet orchards grow,
    And little winds sing softly as they blow
Across the fields where sheep and cattle graze,
    Cooling the heat of sultry summer days,
As the long summer twilight settles down,
    Upon the little houses of the town.

I love flat roads that seem to stretch away
    Beyond the narrow borders of today
Into some never-never land where we
    May find tall castles by a shining sea.
But for today I'll take a quiet field
    With a bright sun above it like a shield.

Photo Opposite
PALOUSE, WASHINGTON
Gene Ahrens

COLLECTOR'S CORNER

Through the genius of American industry, iridescent pressed glass was mass produced in the early 1900s. This reasonably priced glass could be purchased by the working class, which brightened up their homes with colorful, decorative objects.

Carnival Glass, a name coined in the early 1950s by early collectors of iridescent pressed glass, was first advertised in trade journals in 1908, the same year the first mass-produced Ford Model T rolled off the assembly line. Carnival Glass was made in and around the Ohio Valley between 1908 and 1928. Many companies produced Carnival Glass but the six most productive factories were Fenton, Northwood, Dugan, Westmoreland, Imperial, and Millersburg. The glass was for sale in china and glass shops, department stores, and general stores across America. Large quantities of this popular glass were sold overseas as well. As the years passed, the "lesser" or leftover pieces were sold by the barrel to wholesale houses for distribution as prizes to circuses, churches, lodges, and

carnivals—hence the possible origin of its present day name. Carnival Glass is a prominent star of beauty among antiques and collectibles. Its design, color, and shape are unique.

The process of pressing glass began in this country in the early nineteenth century. Basically a "gather" of hot molten glass was dropped into a mold, then pressed with a plunger (the part of the mold that gave the piece its shape). The glass spread out evenly to take the shape and pick up the mold's design. After the pressing process, and while the glass was still hot, it was sprayed with a metallic coating which gave the iridescent finish to the piece.

Carnival Glass once had the nickname "Poor Man's Tiffany." This process of spraying still-hot pressed glass with a metallic coating was the same process used by Tiffany and others to iridize their art glass. The manufacturers of this iridescent pressed glass advertized it as Golden Iris, Egyptian Iridescent, Rubi Gold, and Dragon-blue. These

names all referred to the iridescence, which is the most striking characteristic of Carnival Glass.

Today's collector can find Carnival Glass in a multitude of colors. Collectors refer to the "base glass" color as the color we see when holding a piece to the light. The iridescence is then applied to the base glass color. For example, what collectors know as marigold is a clear glass with selenium and stannous chloride sprayed on it. Its marigold finish may vary greatly according to the chemical mixture of the spray. Other base glass colors are green, blue, purple, red, pastel blue and green, and variations which include opalescent, or milky, edges.

The people who artistically carved designs into hundreds of molds are responsible for the many lovely patterns in Carnival Glass. The Grape and Cable theme was very popular. It can be found in at least twenty-five various designs. Trout and Fly, made by the Millersburg Glass Company, is also popular among collectors.

The manufacturers and their skilled workers

not only went to great lengths to have color and design variety, they did their best to provide a variety of shapes. Punch sets, table sets, water sets, mugs, plates, bowls, vases, and novelty items were among the shapes produced. Some of these sound as though they were made to be used, but most were decorative items only.

Although we say Carnival Glass was mass-produced, the glass workers' skill and tools were involved to individualize each piece. For example, when a mold turned out a shallow bowl, the glass maker could flatten it into a plate, or pull it up into a deep bowl, or ruffle the edges with a special crimping device. When a vase was made, it might be swung into twice the height it would be if left as it came out of the mold. Once in a while a glass worker might squeeze the top of a tumbler to create a spittoon.

Carnival Glass is as lovely today as when it was produced, and it remains an important part of our American glass heritage.

Ruth Schinestuhl

Lace Curtains

Zelma Bomar

In the parlor, long years ago,
Hung lace curtains, white as snow,
With scrolls of flowers and fancy things,
And one could picture angel wings.

Scalloped all around the edge,
They hung from a pole, through wooden pegs.
How proud my mother was to show
Her lace curtains, white as snow.

They were washed with tender care,
Not to snag them anywhere.
Curtain stretchers did the rest
To make them look their very best.

We children dared to touch them not,
For fear of leaving a smudgy spot.
The filtering sun made spots of gold
Through the curtain's dainty folds.

Sometimes I like to reminisce,
Recalling lovely things like this:
In our parlor, long years ago,
Hung lace curtains, white as snow.

Special Moments

G. Alvord-Seale

There are certain special moments
On a gentle summer day,
When the breeze will blow the curtain
In just a certain way,

When the peaceful sounds of summer—
Things forgotten until then—
Drift in through the window
And bring childhood back again.

The slam of a kitchen screen door
Down the street a ways,
The sound of noontime dishes
Being neatly cleaned away;

The rustle of the leaves
When a summer rain starts falling;
The squabble of a mother bird
For her babies calling;

The soft sounds of summer days
Take me to a younger time
When floating gently as a cloud,
All the world was mine.

The Country Trains

Maxine Lyga

What happened to the country trains
    That traveled from town to town?
What happened to the old iron rails
    And the ties that held them down?
What happened to the whistle and
    The big long line of cars?
What happend to the engines, yes,
    I wonder where they are.

And where have all the bad men gone
    Who robbed the trains of old?
Now just their tales are echoed of
    The silver and the gold.
What happened to the depots that
    Stood snug beside the track?
Now we see them falling down,
    And our thoughts go wandering back

To that railroad bed beside the track
    Where once the old train stood;
It's bare of all the telegraph poles
    And the crossarms made of wood.
Remember the old train whistle as
    It echoed through the dells?
I'd like to see those trains once more
    And hear the ringing bells.

But the trains are gone from country towns
    As far as eye can see,
And we reminisce of other days
    When trains made history.
They made this country great and fine,
    Reaching far and wide;
Through hills and dells they cut the trails,
    But alas, they now have died.

Modern times have changed them all,
    They've vanished from our sight,
Except the little electric trains
    That bring children such delight.
Country trains . . . just a memory
    As they reached from shore to shore.
Like the passing of the noble great,
    How we'd like them back once more.

To an Old Desk

Fleta Bruer Gonso

This old worn desk has held for many years
My cherished things—the photographs I love;
Gay, precious yellow letters, bright as tears;
A faded violet; a fragile glove.

In this deep cubicle are laid my schemes
For progress, plotted down in secret gage;
And here are hidden papers filled with dreams
Which sought to spill themselves upon the page.

A crooked line of tiny kitten tracks
Immortalized in India ink march here,
And on the corner, little jagged cracks
Made by small fingers, mischievous and dear.

This old desk, touched by Time's enchanting art,
Becomes an ark of memory for my heart.

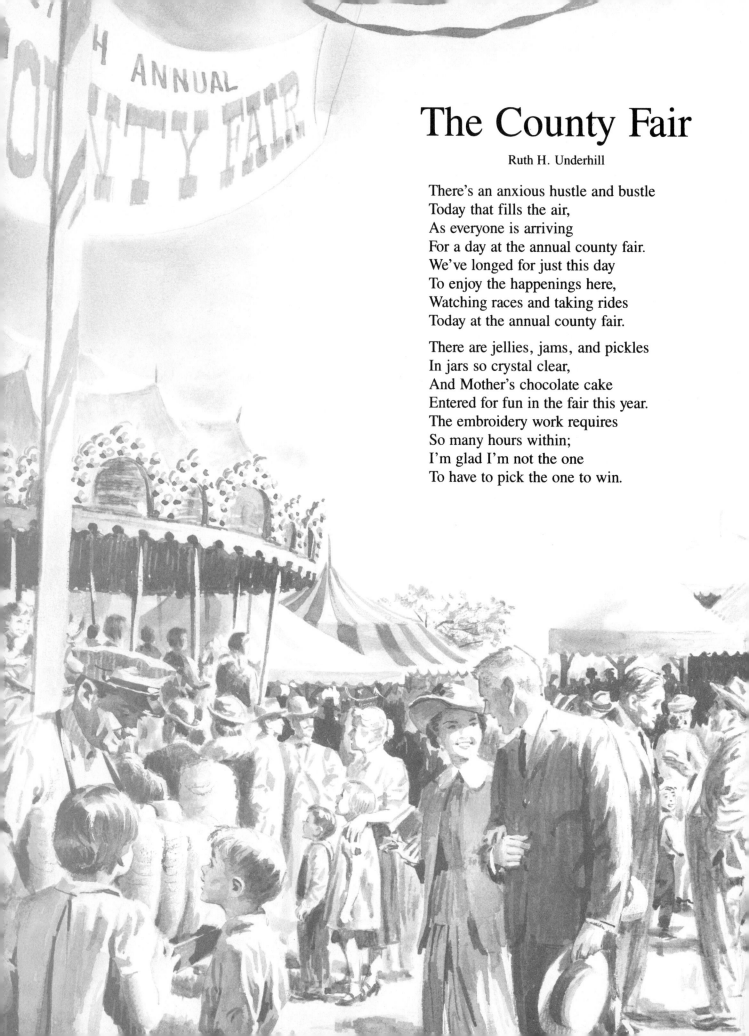

The County Fair

Ruth H. Underhill

There's an anxious hustle and bustle
Today that fills the air,
As everyone is arriving
For a day at the annual county fair.
We've longed for just this day
To enjoy the happenings here,
Watching races and taking rides
Today at the annual county fair.

There are jellies, jams, and pickles
In jars so crystal clear,
And Mother's chocolate cake
Entered for fun in the fair this year.
The embroidery work requires
So many hours within;
I'm glad I'm not the one
To have to pick the one to win.

When it's finally time for lunch,
We dash to the hot dog stand;
What a delightful picnic today
With soda pop in eager hands.
We've ridden the Ferris wheel
And the rhythmic merry-go-round;
We've walked from end to end
Of the bustling busy county fair grounds.

Now as this joyful day
Comes to a happy end,
What's left is memories
As the trampled path we wearily wend.
And they shall live forever
As treasures in our minds,
These memories of the fair
We saw and loved and left behind.

The Millstream

Mildred L. Jarrell

The grand old mill is darkened now;
Still the millstream wanders by,
Caressing the banks and the waterwheel
With a whisper and a sigh.

Time was when the wheel sang its merry song,
And the water gushed and sped,
Sending up crystal drops of spray
As it raced o'er its rocky bed.

Wood ivy and creeper are tangled now,
Hanging over the old mill door;
The creak of the wheel and grinding stones
Are stilled forevermore.

And still the millstream murmurs on,
Soft sounds for the mill to hear,
Reminiscing of times long past,
Memories of yesteryear.

Country Chronicle

Lansing Christman

Old barns are like old scribes. They write a bucolic chronology of life on the farm. Their script is a journal of the seasons, a record of harvests, a narrative of fields.

An aging tobacco barn in Tennessee harbors bundles of large tobacco leaves hanging upside down to dry, white smoke seeping skyward through crevices, the heavy-sweet odor permeating the countryside. A fading red barn

in Wisconsin greets the morning sun as cows trail out slowly to laze away the day. In Nebraska, a farmer opens the barn doors his grandfather fashioned, doors he and his father before him have repaired. Out of the barn that used to house his grandfather's plow horse comes a multi-thousand dollar combine to bring the harvest home.

Some aging barns have been witness to the

comings and goings of time for more than a century. Some have been abandoned to sun and rain, to wind and snow. Still, they depict a rustic elegance when the wilderness starts creeping back to the doors. New trees spring up nearby. Grass and weeds grow and go to seed all around. Vines inside the dark and damp interiors send out tendrils, seeking a foothold in cracks and crevices in their quest for light.

The vintage buildings continue to endure. With sagging skills and loosened boards, with roofs ripped by wind, they are graced with a mellow beauty that is all their own. Standing far back from the road, deserted and alone, they represent generations who followed the plow because they were people of dreams. They were people who loved the soil and chose to live close to it, to nurture and protect it.

Old barns add charm to the pastoral scene of the countryside. They blend in well with the grandeur of the hills. And when I place my hands upon their burnished boards, I sense their antiquity, their origin long ago in a primitive forest of whispering pines.

Time Is a Treasure

Donita Dyer

This day belongs to the world—to rich and poor, to young and old, to commoner and king—time is not a respecter of persons. It keeps company with both renegade and royalty and is bestowed upon us all in the same manner—moment-by-moment, hour-by-hour.

Time is life's greatest asset, a generous gift from the Creator, yet not one hour may be stored for the future. In our affluent society, no one can beg, borrow, or buy an additional day. Even the most fabulous fortune cannot purchase the fleeting moments, or call them back once they are gone.

Time waits for no one. It travels swiftly and in silence, linked with the rising and setting sun. Like a vapor, it is here one moment and gone the next, days disappearing so quickly that we sometimes stand in utter amazement and ask, "Where has the time gone?"

Today is ours—yours and mine—with all the possibilities it offers, twenty-four hours to use as we choose, to spend at our own discretion. What will the day hold? Will we be able to look back and smile with satisfaction, confident that God's gift has not been squandered, or golden opportunities lost forever? If challenges have been met with courage, tasks accomplished to the best of our ability, and warm, meaningful relationships made along the way, then we may say with certainty that this day has been lived to the fullest.

Time is so very precious that we dare not waste a minute. "This is the day which the Lord hath made; we will rejoice and be glad in it." For time is a treasure.

A Slice of Life

Edgar A. Guest

There was a time when Saturday night had a meaning all its own. In the days of my boyhood Saturday had character. It stood out from the rest of the weekdays if not with the solemnity of Sunday, with the distinction of preparations for the Sabbath. So changed are our customs and habits and methods that Saturday is now no different from the other days of the week. Saturday can come and go and scarcely be noticed. What was once "bath night," in city life exists no longer. The invention of rapid heaters has made taking a bath an ordinary matter. One has merely to turn the tap at any hour of the day or night and the bath is ready.

But in the early days the bath was a weekly event. It meant preparation and assignment. It had to be planned so that every member of the family would rise Sunday morning fit for church. This was well enough in the summertime, but in the winter this family rite grew more difficult. The upper floors were cold. The upper rooms were like refrigerators, and so in the severest weather the kitchen was set apart for the ceremony. There beside the comfortable wood or coal stove the tub was placed.

Perhaps those were difficult and trying times, but now they seem to shine among the happiest of my memories. I am not sure that I should like to return to that old-fashioned method, but I do rejoice that it was my privilege to have known it, and I regret that my children will have no such experiences.

I like to get to thinking of the old days that are
    gone,
When there were joys that never more the world
    will look upon,
The days before inventors smoothed the little
    cares away
And made, what seemed but luxuries then, the
    joys of every day;
When bathrooms were exceptions, and we got
    our weekly scrub
By standing in the middle of a little wooden tub.

We had no rapid heaters, and no blazing gas to
    burn,
We boiled the water on the stove, and each one
    took his turn.
Sometimes to save expenses we would use one tub
    for two;
The water brother Billy used for me would also
    do,
Although an extra kettle I was granted, I admit,
On winter nights to freshen and to warm it up a
    bit.

We carried water up the stairs in buckets and in
    pails,
And sometimes splashed it on our legs, and rent
    the air with wails,
But if the nights were very cold, by closing every
    door
We were allowed to take our bath upon the
    kitchen floor.
Beside the cheery stove we stood and gave
    ourselves a rub,
In comfort most luxurious in that old wooden tub.

But modern homes no more go through that
    joyous weekly fun,
And through the sitting rooms at night no half-
    dried children run;
No little flying forms go past, too swift to see
    their charms,
With shirts and underwear and things tucked
    underneath their arms;
The home's so full of luxury now, it's almost like
    a club,
I sometimes wish we could go back to that old
    wooden tub.

Seated in the Back

Elaine Cecil

Among the things that I recall
    From a time when I was small
Are family trips behind the wheel
    Of a shiny automobile

With parents in the front seat,
    Grandparents in the back,
Children squeezed 'tween pairs of legs,
    And a suitcase on the rack.

Years passed and positions changed
    As we children learned to drive;
And the cars themselves increased in
  speed,
    Needing less time to arrive.

With my boyfriend in the front seat,
    I sat closely by his side.
I watched him wash and wax his car
    With ever-glowing pride.

Marriage led to motherhood;
    As babies came along
The sports car soon was traded in
    To accommodate the throng.

With me in the front seat
    And carseats in the rear,
I shuttled noisy children
    Like some modern charioteer.

The chrome is mostly fiberglass
    On the sleek cars of today
As I look into the mirror
    At my hair that's turning gray.

Now my children do the driving
    In a car that has no rack,
And I remember days of long ago
    While seated in the back.

AUTOMOBILES OF THE PAST
Comstock, Inc.

Yesterday's Memory

Susan McGrath

Reflections of one tiny pond
Are flowing through my mind,
Memories of the nearby woods
And things I used to find.

Above the water, calm and blue,
I'd look down to see my face;
The breeze was often whisper light,
Enhancing the pond's pure grace.

Whenever I'm feeling sad and lonely
I think of that tranquil pond,
My happy childhood memory
Of things I grew so fond.

Four-O'Clocks

Hilda Sanderson

Sometimes in the early morning
Before the sun is bright,
There is confusion in our yard
When all is not quite right.

It happens by the backyard fence
Next to the hollyhocks,
Blooming when they aren't supposed to
Are rows of four-o'clocks.

I do not know whose fault it is,
But everyone agrees
Those four-o'clocks should bloom at four,
Instead of when they please.

Popular Music

Craig E. Sathoff

Through ups and downs, good times and bad,
The song has never died.
The popular music of our land
Has lived—a source of pride.

We've sung about America
From lungs filled high with praise.
We've sung of love; we've sung of war.
We've sung of bygone days.

The sheet music, the record shops,
The dancing marathons,
The jukebox in the ice cream shop—
And still the beat goes on.

The bluegrass moods of country folk,
The stirring gospel songs,
The rock, the blues, the old soft-shoe
Have sped the craze along.

This music is America.
Our hearts are joined to sing.
Oh, may we never lose our song,
May freedom ever ring!

Photo Opposite
MUSIC OF LONG AGO
Kuhn Garmon
Comstock, Inc.

Covered Bridge

Kay Hoffman

There's something about a covered bridge
    That's quaint and sweet to see,
Like turning back the page of time
    To the days that used to be.

Far from the clamor of city street
    With its rush and many a scheme,
A covered bridge in the quiet countryside
    Is a place to pause and dream.

You can almost hear the rumble
    Of a carriage drawing nigh,
A ruddy-faced farmer with a wave of his hand
    Calls out a friendly "Hi."

There's something about a covered bridge
    That speaks of simpler days
When people had time to be neighborly
    In quaint old-fashioned ways.

Small-Town Druggist

Craig E. Sathoff

Mortar and pestle, old-time scales,
And bottles and tubes galore,
The small-town druggist is at work
In his well-kept drugstore.

He means so much to all of us
Within our little town.
He serves us so good-naturedly;
His faith in man abounds.

He mingles old-time medicines
With new discoveries
To give each customer the best
Of drugs and remedies.

He has a personal interest in
Each client's malady,
For they are those he knows and loves
In his community.

Bitters and balsams, herbs and salves,
A friendly greeting, too.
The small-town druggist is at work;
He'll do his best for you.

LAABS DRUG STORE

Something Old

Pamela Kennedy

I fingered the folds of my wedding gown as it hung in the dressing room at the church. The silk rustled in hushed whispers, and the sparkling crystals and ivory pearls winked and gleamed at me. This was the day when my dreams would become real. The little girl who had played bride in the backyard, adorned with an organdy curtain, would walk down the aisle, take the hand of her handsome young naval officer, pledge to love and cherish him forever, and begin her new role as a wife. Before me, on the little table, were the traditional bridal accouterments—a pale blue silk garter, an embroidered handkerchief borrowed from my mother, a lovely new pair of pearl earrings, and my "something old," Grandma's locket.

I picked up the necklace and rubbed the smooth, little heart with my fingers, remembering with a smile the day Grandma had given it to me. It was my tenth birthday and I had run down to the two-room flat built under our large old apartment house, to visit the family matriarch.

Grandma opened the door wearing one of her handmade aprons, dusting flour from her hands. Her smile and twinkling blue eyes invited me in before she spoke, and the first questions out of her

mouth were, as always, about food.

"Want a cookie or an apple? I have some nice raisin bread. How about a piece of toast?" Grandma always prefaced every conversation with food. It didn't matter if you were hungry or not, you always said "yes." A "no" elicited questions about your health and digestion, and just wasted time. I agreed to the toast and perched on the high stool Grandma kept by the radiator.

She cut the bread, browned it in her antique toaster, and spread it with creamy butter. Handing the plate to me, she settled into her creaky rocker and eyed me with an impish grin.

"You're ten today," she finally announced as if it were news to me.

"Mmm hmm," I agreed, around a mouthful of raisin toast.

"Well," she said in a conspiratorial tone, "I have something for you." She went to her tiny bedroom and rummaged around in a drawer, tossing out flannel nightgowns, cotton bloomers, and elastic stockings. "Here it is!" she announced victoriously. She came back and handed me a floral print hanky with something tied in the corner. "Open it up!" she said, delighted with herself.

I untied the knot and out slipped the locket. It slithered from my hand and Grandma caught it before it fell.

"Now, this," she said, dangling the golden heart from its fragile chain, "is something I want you to have. Your grandpa ordered this for me from the Sears and Roebuck catalog when we had hardly enough money for food and clothes." She clucked her tongue at the remembrance of the extravagance. "He gave it to me just after your daddy was born. Look here."

Grandma turned the locket over and pointed to some little scratches and dents in the smooth gold of the heart. "Do you know what those are?"

I shook my head and Grandma laughed. "Bite marks! Your daddy used to teethe on this when I rocked him to sleep."

I touched the dents with one tentative finger, trying to imagine my six-foot father as a teething infant. I was taken with a kind of awe, for it was the first time I had ever thought about the past as a personal thing, or seen myself as a part of an ongoing heritage.

Grandma brought me back to the present as she clasped the chain around my neck and patted the locket. "Now you take good care of this and maybe someday you will give it to your grand-daughter."

My ten-year-old imagination couldn't stretch that far, but I touched the locket almost reverently.

The heart-shaped gold locket was a symbol of both past and future and became a special bond between Grandma and me. Now, on my wedding day, I fastened it around my neck again. Grandma couldn't attend the ceremony, being ninety years old and too frail to venture out. I had visited her the day before, however, and told her I would wear the locket, remembering her on my wedding day. She had kissed me then and wished me well, and we had held hands for a time in silence, each recalling the past and contemplating the future.

As I slipped into my wedding dress, Mother helped me adjust the tiny buttons and arrange the billowy veil. My Matron of Honor ticked off the ancient bridal liturgy—something old, something new, something borrowed, and something blue. As the organ began the first chords of Lohengrin, I began the walk into the future accompanied by the richness of the past so beautifully represented by my "something old."

Family Favorites

Basic Pie Crust

Makes two 9-inch single piecrusts or one
9-inch double-crust pie

2¼ cups flour
1 teaspoon salt
¾ cup shortening
8 tablespoons cold water

Sift flour and salt into a large bowl. Cut in shortening with pastry blender or two knives until mixture resembles peas. Add water one tablespoon at a time, mixing lightly with fork until dough holds together. Form dough into a ball; wrap in plastic wrap and chill one hour.

Divide dough in half. Roll out one half on a floured surface until ⅛ inch thick, or about two inches larger than inverted pie pan. Gently ease crust into pie pan.

For single piecrust, trim dough overhang to one inch and flute edges. Fill as directed. For double piecrust, trim dough overhang to ½ inch. Fill as directed. Roll out remaining dough to form top crust. Place top crust over filling. Trim overhang; flute edges. Make several slits near center to allow steam to escape during baking.

Peach Pie

Makes one 9-inch double-crust pie

1 9-inch double piecrust
4 cups peeled and sliced peaches
1½ teaspoons lemon juice
⅔ cup sugar
2 tablespoons flour
½ teaspoon grated lemon peel
½ teaspoon cinnamon
¼ teaspoon nutmeg
⅛ teaspoon salt
1 tablespoon butter, cut into small pieces

Preheat oven to 450° F. Toss peaches and lemon juice together in large bowl. Add remaining ingredients except butter; toss gently. Spoon mixture into bottom crust. Dot with butter. Place top crust over filling; seal and flute edges. Cut slits in crust. Bake at 450° F. for 15 minutes. Reduce heat to 325° F. and bake an additional 20 to 25 minutes or until golden. Cool on rack.

Classic Pecan Pie

Makes one 9-inch single-crust pie

1 9-inch piecrust
½ cup packed light brown sugar
½ cup unsalted butter, soft
¾ cup granulated sugar
3 eggs
¼ teaspoon salt
¼ cup maple syrup
½ cup heavy cream
½ cup coarsely chopped walnuts
½ cup coarsely chopped pecans
½ teaspoon vanilla extract
½ cup pecan halves

Preheat oven to 350° F. In double-boiler top, cream brown sugar and butter until well blended. Add granulated sugar; blend well. Add eggs, one at a time, beating after each addition. Add salt, maple syrup, and cream; mix well. Cook over boiling water, stirring, 5 minutes. Remove from water; stir in the walnuts, chopped pecans, and vanilla. Pour into lined pie plate. Bake 1 hour; arrange pecan halves on top of pie; bake 5 minutes more. Cool.

Note: Pie puffs during baking and shrinks slightly as it cools.

Apple Pie

Makes one 9-inch double-crust pie

1 9-inch double piecrust
6 cups peeled and sliced baking apples
¼ cup light brown sugar
¼ cup granulated sugar
2 tablespoons flour
1 teaspoon cinnamon
½ teaspoon nutmeg
2 tablespoons butter, cut into small pieces
   Milk
   Sugar

Preheat oven to 425° F. Combine apples, sugars, flour, and spices; toss gently. Spoon mixture into bottom crust. Dot with butter. Place top crust over filling; seal and flute edges. Cut slits in crust. Bake at 425° F. for 35 to 40 minutes or until golden. Cool on rack.

Small-Town Street

Donna Ramsey Clark

White picket fences, new-cut grass,
And honeysuckle sweet,
Swings on porches . . . little things
Make up a small-town street.

Neighbors sitting on a porch
To pass the time of day,
Exchanging talk and recipes
In a good old-fashioned way.

Children playing, shouts of glee,
Red wagons, rubber balls,
A spotted dog, an ink-black cat,
Vine-covered garden walls,

Friendly houses, friendly folks—
And here the twain shall meet,
Sharing life as it is lived
Along a small-town street.

Picnic Cloth and Napkins

Ann Marie Braaten

Picnic Cloth Materials:
2½ yards fusible interfacing
½ yard cream broadcloth
½ yard red broadcloth
2½ yards green broadcloth
⅛ yard black broadcloth
1 yard cream poplin
1¼ yards needle punch
Matching thread

Napkin Materials:
2 yards red broadcloth
Matching thread

Picnic Cloth Instructions:
Step One: Cutting Squares and Borders

From the yard of cream poplin cut four squares measuring 17 inches each.

From the green broadcloth cut the following:

One 43½-inch square

Six rectangles measuring 4½ inches by 17 inches

Three rectangles measuring 4½ inches by 43½ inches each

From the needle punch cut one 43½ inch square.

Appliqué Pattern
One square equals one inch.

Step Two: Preparing Appliqués

Press interfacing to the red, cream, remaining green, and black broadcloth.

After drawing watermelon patterns, place each pattern right side down on the interfaced side of the broadcloth. Trace and cut four each of red, cream, and green watermelon sections. Cut 20 black seeds.

Step Three: Appliquéing

Position the green watermelon sections on each of the four 17-inch squares. Pin securely.

Beginning at the flat edge, appliqué the watermelon to the cream square with a wide zigzag stitch having a fine stitch length. Repeat this procedure with the cream and finally the red sections. Appliqué the seeds with a narrower zigzag stitch.

Step Four: Sewing Borders

Stitch a short green strip to one of the cream squares, leaving a ½-inch seam allowance. Stitch a second short strip to the opposite side of the same square. Attach another cream square to this green strip. Lastly sew an additional short strip to the opposite side of this cream square. Repeat this procedure for the remaining cream squares and short green strips.

Using a long green strip, connect the two large patchworked sections, leaving a ½-inch seam allowance. Finish outer edges of patchwork by stitching remaining strips to each edge.

Step Five: Sewing Front to Back

With right side up, place picnic cloth top on the needle punch square. Place the broadcloth square over the picnic cloth. Pin. Leaving a 9-inch opening for turning, stitch around the outside edges, using a ½-inch seam allowance.

Trim corners and turn cloth right side out. Press lightly with a warm iron. Hand sew the opening.

Step Six: Quilting

Lay the picnic cloth flat. Pin around the inside edges of each cream square.

Using the longest straight stitch, machine quilt (topstitch) along the inside edge of each square. It is best to begin at the center and stitch outward to each corner.

Napkin Instructions
Step One: Cutting

Cut four 18-inch squares.

Step Two: Hemming

To form hem press under ¼ inch twice along the outside edges of each square. Miter corners. Machine stitch the hem along the fold.

Photo Opposite
OLD-TIME PICNIC
Nancy Robinson

Old Photographs

Craig E. Sathoff

Old photographs are histories
With powers unsurpassed
For fostering the special joy
Of looking to the past.

The velvet-padded photo book
For years was tucked away,
Until within an attic trunk
It came to light one day.

What fun to turn the pages back
In family history
And see again the old frame house
The way it used to be!

The pillared porch then wound around
The house on two front sides;
A wooden swing hung from the roof;
Clematis vined 'longside.

Although the porch has been removed,
The house is much the same,
With just a touch of comfort gone
Without the old porch swing.

It's really rather strange to see
A look around the eyes
That's similar in Great-grandpa
And our youngest little guy.

It's fun to view the town's Main Street
Parked full of Model T's
And see the boys in the knickers
That reach just to the knees.

Old photographs add unity
And nurture family ties
By adding to the present day
A touch of days gone by.

Old Books

Craig E. Sathoff

I love the splendor of old books
That on each weathered page
Pass all our wisdom, hopes, and dreams
Down to another age.

I love the illustrations, too,
In lithograph and ink
By artists who communicate
In manner most distinct.

I find the children's books most grand
With pictures through and through.
The Chatter Box, The Prattler's Book—
They're filled with wisdom, too.

Each time I pass an antique shop,
I always stop a bit
To see if they have books for sale—
Old gems of charm and wit.

And if they do, you may be sure
I'll linger for awhile,
Then leave with purchase in my hand
And a contented smile.

Old-Fashioned Flowers

Rose Emily Houston

I always plant my flower bed
Along a mossy old stone wall.
Behind it grows an apple tree
Where chiffon blossoms fall.

First I plant the hollyhocks
In skirts of ruffled pinks and reds.
Then the spikes of delphiniums
Lift up their cheerful sky blue heads.
Next, old-fashioned zinnias
Wearing yellow bonnets bright
Bow to kiss transparent silk
Of the stately iris white.

Marigolds from bright orange
To a lovely lemon hue,
And asters of frilly lavender
Are fresh and lightly scented, too.
The tangle of pretty petunias
Lift their trumpets to be heard,
Calling, "Come and share my sweet nectar"
To the hovering, jewel-like hummingbird.

Then I trim the mounded edges
In the brilliance of moss rose,
And with love and tender care,
My old-fashioned flower bed grows.

The Wild Honey Suckle

Philip Freneau

Fair flower, that dost so comely grow,
Hid in this silent, dull retreat,
Untouched thy honied blossoms blow,
Unseen thy little branches greet:
    No roving foot shall crush thee here,
    No busy hand provoke a tear.

By Nature's self in white arrayed,
She bade thee shun the vulgar eye,
And planted here the guardian shade,
And sent soft waters murmuring by;
    Thus quietly thy summer goes,
    Thy days declining to repose.

Smit with those charms, that must decay,
I grieve to see your future doom;
They died—nor were those flowers more gay,
The flowers that did in Eden bloom;
    Unpitying frosts, and Autumn's power
    Shall leave no vestige of this flower.

From morning suns and evening dews
At first thy little being came:
If nothing once, you nothing lose,
For when you die you are the same;
    The space between, is but an hour,
    The frail duration of a flower.

The Shaker Message

Mary Case

"Put your hands to work, and your hearts to God," was the motto exemplified by the group of people known to the world as Shakers. The message is as workable today as it was two hundred years ago.

The Shakers believed in pacifism and perfection, and they practiced this belief in their daily lives. They were a religious group which separated itself from the Quaker Church of England in the mid-1700s. Looking for religious freedom, the small group of eight—led by Mother Ann Lee—came to the colonies in 1774. Their first settlement was in the wilderness near Albany, New York.

For ten years Mother Ann led her growing group, teaching them that it was important to work for the good of all and not for personal gain. Speak-ing on the importance of cleanliness, she said, "Good spirits will not live where there is dirt. There is no dirt in heaven."

The Shakers, whose formal name was The United Society of True Believers in Christ's Second Appearing, practiced some beliefs that were never popular in wider society. For instance they felt that celibacy was mandatory, so the only way their group could grow was by taking in new members, either as adults or as orphans and foundling children. An orphan was cared for and raised in the Shaker community until the age of twenty-one when he or she had to decide whether or not to officially join the Shakers or "return to the world."

Shakers were a communal sect. That is, they

lived and worked together in small communities as families, sharing the work and sharing the rewards.

For about a hundred years they grew in numbers, and several communities were established in the Northeast. By the mid-1800s, there were 6,000 practicing Shakers living in twenty-one communities from Maine to Florida and west to Kentucky and Indiana.

Whatever work the Shakers did was to them a form of worship, a way of communing with God. If they were farmers, their barns and tools were as neat as humanly possible. Their farming became well known during these years and the people of "the world," that is, anyone not Shaker, began to buy their seeds and their products. Later their herb medicines became as popular as their active seed business.

It's important to realize that over a hundred years ago there weren't doctors in every town, but there were traveling medicine men selling worthless concoctions reputed to relieve every ailment from head to toe. Into this environment came the Shakers quietly selling their pure and healthful cures. There are records showing that many of their painkillers were used during the Civil War.

When the Shakers lacked something, they made it. When they thought of a new and better way to do something, they developed the tools to make it happen. They are credited with inventing the clothespin, the flat broom, an automatic apple parer, the first metal pen point, a revolving oven, a washing machine, the buzz saw, and numerous other things which made their jobs easier or their products better.

Shaker furniture was made with plain and simple lines, reflecting their beliefs in simple living and quality crafting. Catalogs are still available showing some of their furniture which was for sale, including their still-sought-after chairs with woven tape seats. They even developed a tilting chair foot. This was a device in the bottom of the back legs of a chair which allowed the person sitting in it to lean back without damaging the carpet or the floor. Their baskets, their clocks, and their fine needlework became recognized by outsiders who bought them, often in large quantities to sell to others.

In many ways, they were ahead of their time.

Eldress Bertha Lindsay tells of having electricity in their Canterbury, N.H., community by 1910 and their first automobile in 1908.

And then the Shakers began to die out, until today there are only two communities left in the United States. Former Shaker villages are being restored, but active communities of Shakers are now only in Maine and New Hampshire.

There is much we can admire in the Shakers: their simple life, their harmony with others, their self-subsistence, and, especially, their belief in the importance of doing each job in the very best way.

We can still learn from Shakers such as Eldress Bertha who told a group of visitors to her community that Shakers were very human and did not always agree. "But," she said, "when we had disagreements we would settle them with each other before sunset." In the morning, then, the sun always rose on opportunities for harmony and perfection within the finiteness of God's world.

The Old Hometown Quartet

Robert Donald Foss

It wasn't perfect harmony, and yet I can't forget
The brand of music furnished by the Old Hometown Quartet.

Whatever the occasion—from a picnic to a fair—
The day was never quite complete without the quartet there.
When excitement faded and the kids began to fret,
We called for a "selection" by the Old Hometown Quartet.

Jim Johnson sang the tenor, and he sang it through his nose,
While his lengthy Adam's apple seemed to bob up from his toes;
But when the pitch was sounded and each one took up his part,
That nasal tenor tightened all the drawstrings 'round your heart!

Harve Haley was the leader, and (like Harve) his voice was thin;
'Twas hard to hear the melody above the noise and din.
But in the softer moments, before the piece was through,
You'd hear old Harvey leading—in accents sweet and true.

The baritone was Obermyer; he always sang "by ear."
The symbols of the music sheet to him were never clear.
But when it came to blending with Jim's or Haley's note,
The tone that Obermyer produced came from a golden throat.

Ben Jacobs was the basso, and he was so big and round,
No wonder that his deepened tones were always so profound.
Ben somehow scrouged his lips around to reach the deepest bass.
You wondered if he sang most with his throat or with his face!

But taken all together when the quartet sang its tune,
Whether excerpts from a hymnal or a lyric to the moon,
It loosened up the fibers that stretch across your chest,
And brought that glorious feeling of peacefulness and rest.

The old quartet has vanished in the dust of long ago.
Today we get our music brought by the radio
With news of strife and conflict that fill the troubled years
And bring us doubt and anguish, and undiluted fears.

And so I sometimes wonder, 'mid this carnage and this strife,
Just how far we have progressed above the simple life.
Perhaps we would live better and be safer, saner all
If we could pause and listen to the old quartet enthrall!

That Old Shade Tree

Gwenda Isaac Jennings

So many quiet hours I spent
Up in that old shade tree;
Just the shiny whispering leaves,
The sky, fresh air . . . and me.

I sometimes was a queen to rule
(In peaceful wandering dreams)
The world spread out beneath my feet
And inflict my many schemes.

I sailed the vast and foreign seas
In ships to far-off lands.
I piloted my own airplane—
The tire swing named Command.

I battled many battles where
I figured, fought, and won.
That old shade tree and youthful me,
We touched the setting sun.

I felt rain upon my upturned face,
Slid down a pink rainbow,
Felt sorry for those on the ground,
Unluckies far below.

Yes, I had the perfect place
In which to hide and rest,
A place to call my very own;
It passed the childhood test.

It's standing just the same today,
Offering dreams and security.
I hope others one day will say
"That old shade tree . . . and me."

Photo Opposite
BACKYARD SWING
Robert Hayes

August Song

Marion Crook

I love the month of August,
Her gentle, tranquil hours,
The bounty of her gardens,
The brightness of her flowers.

I love to sit at sundown—
When shadows stretch out long
Across the new-mown hayfields—
And hear the peeper's song.

I love her fruits and berries,
Her picnics and her fairs,
The moments for relaxing
From all our worldly cares.

I love the month of August,
And I cherish every day,
For I know that soon our summer
Will have softly slipped away.

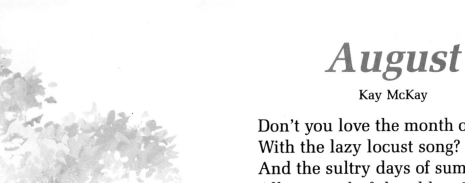

August

Kay McKay

Don't you love the month of August
With the lazy locust song?
And the sultry days of summer
All so wonderful and long?

To walk across a field of grass
That's parched by noonday sun
Makes a kind of hidden music
Touching hearts of old and young.

While thirsty roses cry for rain
And corn fields, too, need more,
Sunflowers nod their golden heads
Beside the cellar door.

Then when the rain comes pelting down
Kids scoot for porches neat,
Catching running water from the eaves
On outstretched small, bare feet.

The eventide brings rainbows,
Nature's glory to behold,
Of purple, gold, vermillion—
A color riot bold.

All the months have beauty and
A time for play and rest,
But don't you really, truly think
That August is the best?

Photo Overleaf
GLACIER NATIONAL PARK
Larry Burton

I Remember a Town

Sheila Stinson

I remember a town and a pleasant street
Where the maple trees flung high
Their shading branches through summer days
Beneath a calm blue sky.

I remember the children who ran and played
On corners beneath the lights,
Their shrill young voices gay and sweet,
Those quiet starlit nights.

I shall always remember the popcorn man
And the concerts in the square,
Kindly faces of those I loved;
I almost see them there.

I remember a man with warm brown eyes
In a little grocery store,
Who for my penny always gave
Six chocolates, sometimes more.

I remember a town, though the years are long
And miles lie between;
A town that is dearest to my heart
Of all the towns I've seen.

Split Rail Fences

Laurie Wilcox

The split rail fences on our farm
Gave the home place lots of charm;
Up the hills and down the vales
They seemed to run on zigzag rails.

The pastures green were fenced around
Where herds of cattle could be found
Quietly grazing and now and then,
Lowing softly in the glen.

The fence to us meant play and fun,
And watching lizards in the sun,
And sniffing honeysuckles sweet
That climbed the railed trellis neat.

The split rail fence had a grayish hue
And soon would be replaced, we knew.
What pioneer with love and duty
Had split the rails for farmland beauty?

The Road to

Let's go along together
Down the road to yesterday,
To live again the memories
That years have stored away.
In Grandpa's horse and buggy
We shall drive into the town,
The buggy black and shining,
And the horse a chestnut brown.
Our first stop is for candy
From our childhood days of yore,
With Dobbins at the hitching post
Outside the country store.

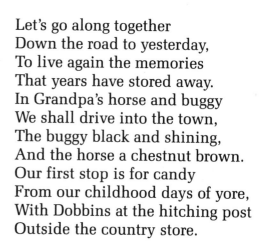

The next stop is the druggist—
In the window, hanging high,
Is that fancy glass container
That we wanted so to buy;
All full of colored liquid
To sparkle in the light,
Though told it held no perfume
We always thought it might.
Inside we'll get a soda,
Where the marble counter's cool;
We feel a bit important
Seated high upon the stool.

Yesterday

Now we're by the barbershop
With its pole of red and white;
We used to swing around it
In a youthful, keen delight.
We stop now at the corner
To allow our horse a drink
From a horse trough made of iron
Filled with water to the brink.
Now Grandpa makes a purchase
At a small tobacco store,
Where we see the wooden Indian
That stands beside the door.

It's time we're turning homeward
And Grandpa lets us drive.
The oil lamp will be lighted
By the time that we arrive.
The porch step has a scraper
Where we stop to clean our shoes,
Impatient to be inside
Telling Mother all the news.
We find her in the kitchen
Baking loaves of fragrant bread;
We'll have some with our supper
Then it's time we're off to bed.

                    Harriet Whipple

Photo Overleaf
COLORADO NATIONAL MONUMENT
Gene Ahrens

Green River

William Cullen Bryant

When breezes are soft and skies are fair,
I steal an hour from study and care,
And hie me away to the woodland scene,
Where wanders the stream with waters of green,
As if the bright fringe of herbs on its brink
Had given their stain to the waves they drink;
And they, whose meadows it murmurs through,
Have named the stream from its own fair hue.

Yet pure its waters—its shallows are bright
With colored pebbles and sparkles of light,
And clear the depths where its eddies play,
And dimples deepen and whirl away,
And the plane tree's speckled arms o'ershoot
The swifter current that mines its root,
Through whose shifting leaves, as you walk the hill,
The quivering glimmer of sun and rill
With a sudden flash on the eye is thrown,
Like the ray that streams from the diamond stone.
Oh, loveliest there the spring days come,
With blossoms, and birds, and wilk-bees' hum;
The flowers of summer are fairest there,
And freshest the breath of the summer air;
And sweetest the golden autumn day
In silence and sunshine glides away.

Dreaming

Florence M. DeLong

In summer when the air is soft and warm,
I love to sit beside a quiet stream
And let my worldly cares all slip away—
Then I am free to rest a while and dream.
I dream about the maple tree back home—
Oh, how we loved to linger in its shade
And listen to the songbirds high above
Who blest us with their daily serenade.

I look about me now, and through the mist
Beyond the distant shore, I think I see
That all the trees in slow procession there
Are moving toward the water—and to me!
Is this a fantasy or is it real?
And why should trees forsake their native home
To search for water, like the wandering deer
And other woodland creatures meant to roam?

Then suddenly a voice within me says:
"This is a dream; all dreams will fade away."
Yes, that is true, but for a little while
They lend enchantment to a summer's day.

Capture the Magic of Autumn with *Ideals*

You look up in the sky one day to see a flock of birds flying south, and suddenly you realize that autumn has arrived. The trees soon dress themselves in brilliant hues. The leaves are dancing with the blustering wind, falling and whirling around, forming great shifting mounds.

Ideals captures it all. In our next issue, *Autumn Ideals,* we will bring you the soaring migration of birds, the age-old rhythm of school opening, the changing colors of leaves, the welcome playfulness of Halloween—and the best photography and illustration anywhere. All for you.

We know that Mrs. Mae E. Thompson of Suncook, New Hampshire is looking forward to the next issue. She writes:

> *I have been so pleased with my copies of* Ideals . . . *I have some old copies . . . These are my treasures. I often reread them . . . and whatever holiday or season, I go back to my* Ideals . . . *the current* Ideals *are worthy of keeping as my treasures now.*

Thank you Mrs. Thompson. We like to know we are bringing all our readers the beauty and celebration of life in each colorful issue. We hope you enjoy *Autumn Ideals*. And for a special gift to a friend, how about *Ideals?*

ACKNOWLEDGMENTS

FLAT LAND and OLD HOUSE by Edna Jaques from *THE GOLDEN ROAD*, copyright 1953 by Thomas Allen, Limited, CANADA. Used by permission; excerpt from the book *STILL-MEADOW DAYBOOK* by Gladys Taber. Copyright © 1955 by Gladys Taber. Copyright renewed © 1983 by Constance Taber Colby. Reprinted by permission of Harper & Row, Publishers, Inc. Our sincere thanks to the following whose addresses we were unable to locate: Donna Ramsey Clark for SMALL-TOWN STREET; Marion Crook for AUGUST SONG; Florence M. DeLong for DREAMING; Robert Donald Foss for THE OLD HOMETOWN QUARTET; Fleta Bruer Gonso for TO AN OLD DESK; Rosaline Guingrich for GENERAL STORE; Gwenda Issac Jennings for THAT OLD SHADE TREE; Sheila Stinson for I REMEMBER A TOWN.